THE COMPOSER

The Composer

MICHAEL HURD

London
OXFORD UNIVERSITY PRESS
NEW YORK TORONTO
1968

Oxford University Press, Ely House, London W.1

GLASGOW NEW YORK TORONTO MELBOURNE WELLINGTON
CAPE TOWN SALISBURY IBADAN NAIKOBI LUSAKA ADDIS ABABA
BOMBAY CALCUTTA MADRAS KARACHI LAHORE DACCA
KUALA LUMPUR HONG KONG TOKYO

Printed in Great Britain

CONTENTS

ACKNOWLEDGMENTS

I have quoted at places in the book from the following works: *A Composer's World*, by Paul Hindemith (Harvard University Press and Oxford University Press), *Some Thoughts on Beethoven's Choral Symphony*, by Ralph Vaughan Williams (Oxford University Press), *The Letters of Mozart and His Family*, translated by Emily Anderson (Macmillan), *On Receiving the First Aspen Award*, by Benjamin Britten (Faber & Faber), and *British Composers in Interview*, by Murray Schafer (Faber & Faber). The first and last of these books are of the utmost importance to anyone wishing to pursue the subject in greater depth.

I am most grateful to the publishing staff of the Oxford University Press Department of Music, and the publishing, printing, and engraving staffs of Novello & Company Ltd, for answering my questions with unflagging patience.

The photograph on p. 22 is by Clive Stratt, on pp. 69 and 71 by George Pickow, and on p. 77 by Tom Shanahan; the passages from *Egdon Heath* are reproduced by courtesy of Miss Imogen Holst, the illustration on p. 39 by courtesy of Peters Edition, on p. 43 by courtesy of the Trustees of the British Museum, on p. 44 by courtesy of the BBC, on p. 48 by courtesy of the Performing Right Society, and on 36 by courtesy of the Oxford University Press.

1 · *The Composer*

ALL over the world there are men and women who write music. Nobody has ever bothered to count them, though their number must certainly run into thousands. Of course, only a handful are at all well known, even in their own countries, and only one or two will go down in musical history. But the remainder still have reason enough to call themselves composers: they write music which is published and performed.

It is unlikely, however, that you have one of them as your next-door neighbour. Indeed, so few people meet composers in the ordinary course of events that they are apt to form all kinds of strange ideas about what they are actually like. Pictures of distraught musicians tearing their hair in a frenzy of inspiration are what most people carry in their mind's eye. And nothing could be further from the truth.

If there is anything unusual about the composer it is not to be found in his looks or in the way he behaves. Sit him down with bank managers or research chemists and you would never know the difference. It is only his cast of mind that is unusual.

The composer is a man who can express himself in terms of music. To him it is a language, with rules of its

9

own and its own inner logic. It is not, however, the kind of language that can express ordinary, everyday matters. The ideas that concern music belong to music alone, and can only be understood in musical terms. To the composer their meaning is crystal clear. 'The thoughts which are expressed to me by music that I love,' wrote Mendelssohn, 'are not too indefinite to be put into words, but, on the contrary, too definite.'

There are many 'languages' of this kind in daily use. Each serves a particular field of thought and is adapted to its special needs—the language of science, for example, or of mathematics. The formula $E = mc^2$ may not mean much to the musician, but to Einstein and his colleagues it perfectly expressed a revolution in scientific thought.

The language of music, however, is not quite so straightforward as the language of science. Besides expressing purely musical thoughts, it is also able to suggest quite definite emotions. And, with a little help from words or drama, it can even be made to paint pictures and tell stories. It is from this aspect of music that so many misunderstandings spring.

Music is not itself emotion. But it is capable of awakening in the listener strong recollections of an emotion he already knows. The composer Paul Hindemith has pointed out that if the emotions that music arouses were *real* feelings

. . . they could not change as rapidly as they do; they would not begin and end precisely with the musical stimulus that aroused them. If we experience a real feeling of grief—that is, grief not caused or released by music—it is not possible to replace it, at a moment's notice and without plausible cause, with a feeling of wild gaiety; gaiety, in turn, cannot be replaced by complacency after a fraction of a second. Real feelings need a certain interval of time to develop, reach their climax, and fade again; reactions to music, however, may change as fast as musical phrases do . . .

The romantic idea of a composer at work (Rouget de Lisle composing 'La Marseillaise'). For the reality see page 22.

Yet these feelings can seem so real that people are often tricked into believing that music and emotion are the same thing, and thus they run in grave danger of misunderstanding music altogether.

With music that deliberately sets out to be descriptive or story-telling the situation is just as uncertain. Take any piece of music with a title—*A Storm at Sea*, for example. It may seem as perfect and exact a description as you could wish. But you can be quite sure that if the composer had decided to call the piece *A Fit of Rage* or *The Kettle Boils Over*, you would have found it equally convincing. The fact is that half the work has been done by the title. Vaughan Williams, writing about film music, says, quite bluntly:

. . . you must not be horrified if you find that a passage which you intended to portray the villain's mad revenge has been used by the musical director to illustrate cats being driven out of the dairy. The truth is that within limits any music can be made to fit any situation.

It would seem, then, that we are on dangerous ground when we try to make music act as a substitute for words, drama, pictures, or emotions. And although most composers would admit that it has the power to evoke all these things, they would most of them declare that music's true function is to be logical in purely musical terms. The language of music is the language of music.

Once we have understood this, it becomes easier to reject the popular notion of the composer as a wild, demented creature in the grip of uncontrollable and inexplicable inspiration. Wild, demented composers there may have been. But their wildness has usually had little to do with the fact that they were composers. Without the accident of their musical gifts they would probably have made equally wild and demented brick-layers, or lorry-drivers.

Let us think of the composer as a perfectly ordinary man, to whom fate has given a mind that responds profoundly and creatively to the language we call music. He may perhaps seem a little preoccupied when we meet him in the street, but no more so than any man with an absorbing interest. He will not wear his hair noticeably longer than is the fashion, nor will his eyes be lit with an unearthly glow. In fact, we shall probably walk straight past him.

2· The Composer's Mind

WHEN a work of art moves us profoundly and seems full of meaning, we shall probably say that it is inspired, and that the artist who created it is a man of genius.

Such words—inspired, genius, and the like—are vague and unsatisfactory. They explain nothing, yet we use them continually as if they explained everything. It is almost as if we prefer the mystery they conceal to any more workaday solution that common sense may suggest.

And because music is more remote from everyday life than writing or painting (most people, after all, can write a letter or make a sketch), the composer is the artist most likely to seem 'inspired' and inexplicable. Inspiration comes, apparently, and ideas flow from his pen without effort or anxiety. It is a pleasant picture, but not quite true to life. What goes on in the composer's workshop is, as we shall see, rather different.

How, then, does the composer's mind work?

Alas, we must begin by admitting that there are some things we do not know and may never be able to find out. We do not know what it is that makes a man's mind sensitive to music in the first place. Nor what it is that gives some men that extra sensitivity that enables them to create music of their own. Some combination, perhaps, of the

14

body chemicals? We cannot be sure. The miracle is, to all intents and purposes, a happy accident, and we must accept it as such.

We cannot even turn to the idea of heredity for an explanation. A few great composers have sprung from a long line—Johann Sebastian Bach is the outstanding example—and some, like Mozart, have been the children of gifted musicians. But at least an equal number have arrived quite unheralded by family tradition: a surprise to themselves and an embarrassment to their parents.

The composer's mind is fertile soil in which the seeds of new music may be cultivated. But where do the seeds come from? To answer this question we must turn to common-sense guess-work.

To begin with: ideas do not spring out of thin air. This is quite unthinkable. Everything in this world has a source, and in the case of the composer it seems obvious that his ideas are based upon what other composers have done before him.

Think of it like this: fate makes the composer's mind peculiarly receptive to musical impressions. From the moment he is born his mind begins to hoard each musical experience that comes its way. His mind, in fact, becomes a vast reference library of musical ideas, of which he may be only dimly aware.

Imagine that each of these musical ideas can be broken down into its simplest parts—just as you might break down a word into its separate letters. Each part is meaningless by itself. Imagine, then, that each of these basic parts is provided with a hook and an eye, so that they can be linked together in any order. The composer's mind can now be seen as the uniquely sympathetic atmosphere in which such linking together can be accomplished.

We can now begin to form some idea of what it is that distinguishes the musical mind from the unmusical one. In the unmusical mind there may well be a small number of musical ideas stored away, but the atmosphere is unsympathetic and no links can be made. In the second-rate

Sketches by Gustav Holst for *Egdon Heath*.

musical mind the ideas can be made to join in logical fashion, but only in a secondhand way. The result is simply an obvious re-hash of other men's thoughts. In the first-rate musical mind—the one that has 'genius'—the links are made in an entirely novel and completely convincing manner, and thus emerge with an authority of their own.

There is more to it than this, however. What we have described takes place, for the most part, at the deepest levels of the composer's unconscious mind. Above, sitting

Part of *Egdon Heath* in full score, showing how the sketches have been used.

alert and in judgement, is his conscious mind, fortified to the limits of his taste and experience. Each musical idea must pass this rigorous censor, or be rejected.

Very often the new patterns that a great composer has to offer will surprise and even shock other men and women. They will seem too revolutionary, too far removed from the accepted music of the age. But after a time it will become obvious that the new music is held together by links that are strong and logical, and then it too will sink into the vast reservoir of tradition.

For proof that the composer's mind constantly creates a new kind of order out of old materials, we need only consider the way in which he learns his craft in the first place.

Composers learn to compose simply by composing. Inevitably, they begin, even the greatest and most naturally gifted of them, by imitating the composers they most admire. Sometimes they copy great masters, but equally the work of lesser men can help and inspire them. Once they have learned to handle the materials of music with confidence, they will become more and more adventurous. Their personality will begin to assert itself, so that they are no longer content to imitate but are driven instead to create their own kind of music. What they now write will reflect their particular way of looking at life, and will bear the hall-marks of an individual style that other men will recognize and honour.

Why should a man put himself to all this trouble merely to create a few works in his own image? It cannot be for the money—there are easier ways of acquiring that. It is hardly ever for the glory—this, if it comes, will seem irrelevant.

The genuine composer is compelled by some inner force. He can neither explain nor control it. All he knows is that if he does not make use of his talents he will be miserable. The need to create boils up in him like steam in a kettle. If there is no outlet he will explode.

Sometimes this urge is a form of compensation for something the composer feels to be unsatisfactory in his life or personality. He creates a new world as a refuge from the one he does not like. The neurotic Tchaikovsky, for example, declared that he would have gone mad had it not been for music.

But more often the composer simply shares the need that all mankind is dogged by: to find something that gives a meaning and purpose to life—something that is larger and more glorious than the mere fact of being alive. To some it may be the raising of a family, or the ambition to build a business empire. It may lie in deeply-held religious beliefs, or cherished political convictions. Mountains are climbed because of it, and oceans braved single-handed. To the born composer it takes a special form: the need to create music.

3 · *The Composer at Work*

THERE is no one method of composing. Composers work in different ways, entirely according to temperament. Some like to improvise at the piano, jotting down ideas as they go. Some like to work out their ideas on paper, going over them again and again until they reach a satisfactory shape. Some prefer to do all the work in their heads, only picking up a pen to write down the finished piece. And some, perhaps the majority, combine all three approaches.

Whichever method you adopt, composing calls for enormous powers of concentration. In the most convincing works the musical ideas follow each other so logically that it would be impossible to improve upon a single note. We feel that the composer's mind has never for a moment wandered from the musical argument. He has given it the whole of his attention.

A remarkable instance of this ability to focus the mind on musical composition is recorded in one of Mozart's letters:

I send you herewith a prelude and a three-part fugue. The reason why I did not reply to your letter at once was that on account of the wearisome labour of writing these small notes, I could not finish the composition any sooner. And, even so, it is awkwardly done, for the prelude ought to come first and the fugue to follow. But I composed the fugue first and wrote it down while I was thinking out the prelude.

Mozart was a composer who liked to work out ideas in his head before committing them to paper. This meant that he could be composing all the time—even when walking about the streets, or eating a meal. And from this letter it would seem that he was also able to split his mind into watertight compartments, using one level to carry out routine musical matters while the other got on with the serious business of creation. Without this capacity for complete concentration it is difficult to see how he could have written so much music in so short a lifetime.

Beethoven, on the other hand, did much of his work on paper, making endless sketches until he was satisfied with every detail. Fortunately some of his notebooks have survived, and we can trace the immense struggle that took place as he created his music. Often a theme that sounds simple and inevitable, like the spontaneous song of a bird, came into existence only after many poorer versions had been thrown away. Indeed, some of the early attempts are so crude and unpromising that they seem more like the work of a bungling amateur than a man of genius. What they represent, of course, is Beethoven's effort to pin down an idea that had flashed through his mind in an instant. The first sketch succeeds in catching only the vague outline. The sketches that follow then read like a heroic chase through the imagination, until the ideal is finally recaptured.

Beethoven's sketchbooks provide a clue as to how *inspiration* takes place. Composers will tell you that the first warning they have of a new work is often not so much a particular musical idea, as a sudden knowledge of what the work will be like when it is finished. They must then carry this musical vision in their minds, while they struggle to achieve it, painfully piecing together the ingredients that will make it a reality. It is as if a jeweller had dreamed of a magnificent necklace and, on waking, had set about the task of finding the right gems and cutting and polishing them until his dream came true.

Of course, complete musical ideas can also crop up in the composer's mind. And when this happens he will know

Benjamin Britten at work.

instinctively (as the result of long experience) what kind of work they are best suited for. The musical idea that will fit the delicate textures of a string quartet will be very different from one that will go to make a symphony; and both will be as different again from the tune that is at home in a ballet score. Each idea has its own personality, its own musical weight. Only the inexperienced or inadequate composer will mistake the nature of the material he is using and try to force it along unsuitable lines.

Because it is so necessary to keep a firm grip on the overall shape of a piece of music, many composers like to sketch their works in 'short score'. Regardless of whether the music is for voices, orchestra, or anything else, they jot down a rough outline on two or three staves—such as might easily be played on the piano. Once this general impression has been written down they can then go back and complete the details—working, perhaps, for many months on an outline that may have taken only a few hours to set down. Here is Tchaikovsky's account of his sketching methods:

I usually write my sketches on the first piece of paper that comes to hand. I jot them down in the most abbreviated form. A melody never stands alone, but invariably has the harmonies that belong to it. These two elements of music, together with the rhythm, cannot be separated; every melodic idea brings its own inevitable harmony and its appropriate rhythm. If the harmony is very intricate, I set down in the sketch a few details on the working out of the parts; when it is quite simple, I put in only the bass, or a figured bass, and sometimes not even this. If the sketch is intended for an orchestral work, the ideas appear ready-coloured by some special instrumental combination.

This stage of composition—the sketch—is remarkably pleasant and interesting. It brings an indescribable delight; accompanied, however, by a kind of unrest and nervous agitation. Sleep is disturbed and meals forgotten.

Tchaikovsky's remarks about the excitement and nervous tensions that go with creative activity are borne out by the experience of many composers. Ordinary time will seem to stand still, and the facts of daily life will mean nothing. Obsessed with his work, the composer may even find that he cannot afterwards remember exactly how it was accomplished. This part of creative work is like a trance: a state of high exhilaration, in which the artist is lifted right out of himself and made oblivious to everything around him.

But the intoxication cannot last for ever. What follows is the sober business of perfecting the detailed score. And for this task the composer needs a clear head and every ounce of craftsmanship he can muster. Nothing can be left to chance. When he has written down the last note it is other men who must perform the music, and if he has not made his intentions clear he cannot expect them to guess what was in his mind.

Work on a large scale—a symphony, say, or an opera—may take many months, even years. Here the wonder is that the composer can make his music seem all of a piece, so that it sounds as if it took no longer to write than it does to perform. Somehow he must be able to keep the vision of the complete work steadily before him, while he moves towards it with craft and ingenuity. No wonder composers complain that the sustained effort of writing a major work can leave them exhausted and even physically ill.

4 · *The Composer's Workshop*

THOUGH they may not run from nine to five, composing has its office hours like any other job. So much of what the composer does is sheer hard work, that it is absolutely essential for him to establish some kind of order—some habit of work—if he is to get anything done at all. The stories of Schubert gossiping with his friends in a café and then breaking off for a moment to scribble some masterpiece on the nearest menu illustrate the exception rather than the rule.

Odd as it may seem, the mere fact of sitting down at the same desk, in the same room, and at the same hour each day of the week can stimulate the composer's thoughts. 'I am sitting,' he feels, 'in the place where I work. Why then, I had better do something.' And, with luck, ideas begin to flow.

Here is Benjamin Britten's view of the matter:

I only write while I am at home in Aldeburgh. I believe strongly in a routine. Generally I have breakfast at eight o'clock and am at work before nine, working through until quarter past one. Then I have a break with a walk before returning to work from five until eight again.

Mozart, writing to his sister in 1782, paints a similar picture:

My hair is always done by six o'clock in the morning and by seven I am fully dressed. I then compose until nine. From nine to one I give lessons. Then I lunch, unless I am invited to some house where they lunch at two or even three o'clock, as for example today at Countess Zichy's and Countess Thun's. I can never work before five or six o'clock in the evening, and even then I am often prevented by a concert. If I am not prevented I compose until nine.

... As I cannot rely on being able to compose in the evening, owing to the concerts which are taking place and also to the uncertainty as to whether I may not be summoned now here and now there, it is my custom (especially if I get home early) to compose a little before going to bed. I often go on writing until one—and am up again at six.

There, are, of course, moments when a composer will feel impelled to compose whatever the circumstances—as Johann Strauss's barber had reason to remember:

When I shaved Herr von Strauss he would often jump up from his seat and rush to the piano to play a few measures, then take one of the pencils that were lying around and write down a few notes.

Sometimes composing habits verge on superstition. Haydn, for example, is said always to have worn a ring given him by the King of Prussia whenever he wanted to compose an especially fine work. And as a matter of course he never began to compose without first praying for help and guidance.

Wagner, on the other hand, placed his faith in having the right kind of atmosphere to compose in:

I cannot live like a dog. I cannot sleep on straw and refresh myself with bad wines. My excitable, delicate, ardently craving and uncommonly soft and tender sensibility must be coaxed in some way if my mind is to accomplish the horribly difficult task of creating a non-existent world.

He therefore commanded rooms draped in silks and satins, heavy with delicate perfumes, and disported himself in clothes to match. (Moreover, he invariably found someone who was willing to foot the bill.)

Most composer's demands are not quite so extravagant. A room, a desk, a piano, and above all—peace and quiet. But this last simple and utterly essential requirement may be the most difficult to come by, as Mozart found in 1771:

Upstairs we have a violinist, downstairs another one, in the next room a singing master who gives lessons, and in the room opposite ours an oboist. This is good fun when you are composing! It gives you plenty of ideas.

Meyerbeer once solved a similar problem by renting three apartments, and then only using the one in the middle!

Many composers find that improvisation helps to stimulate the musical imagination. This does not mean that they sit at the piano picking out tunes with one finger and writing them down one note at a time, as composers always seem to do in popular films. Rather, it is the sheer sound of music that helps induce the kind of mood in which creation can take place. It is as if the composer were playing himself in, generating an atmosphere that will bring his mind round to the point of true concentration. Here is Wagner, speaking of his piano as if it were a beloved friend:

The piano has just arrived, been unpacked and set up . . .
this wondrous, soft, sweet, melancholy instrument wooed me
back to music once more.

Not every composer has felt quite so enthusiastic, however. Some have denounced pianos outright. Weber, for
example:

The composer who secures his ideas from the piano is almost
always born poor and on the way to yielding up his spirit to
the ordinary and vulgar. Those very hands, with their damned
piano-fingers, their eternal practising and mastering, finally
acquire a sort of independence of their own.

. . . How differently he creates whose inner ear has become
the sole judge of his imagination!

Obviously there is much in Weber's warning. The hands
at the keyboard can easily dictate the course of musical invention. But the odds are evenly divided: composers who
have used the piano have written music as great and lasting
as those who have scorned it.

The means by which composers have tried to stimulate
their imaginations are scarcely to be numbered. Some, like
Beethoven, have found inspiration in long country walks.
Mozart frequently worked at a musical problem while
playing billiards. Britten, we are told, can plan his music
while sitting in the back of a car, or riding in a train.

In each case, what the composer is doing is to indulge
in a simple activity that distracts the conscious part of his
mind, while leaving the deeper levels free to ponder musical
problems. In a grander sort of way he is doing exactly
what the ordinary man does when he decides to weed the
garden and 'think things out'.

Of all stimuli one of the most effective is surely the

pressure of time: the need to get the job finished by a certain date, come what may. Rossini, advising a young composer on the best way to write an overture, had no doubts about this:

Wait until the evening before the opening night. Nothing primes inspiration more than necessity, whether it be the presence of the copyist waiting for your work, or the prodding of

Beethoven's study. This picture was painted immediately after Beethoven's death, but probably shows the usual condition of the room – he was never tidy in his habits.

an impresario tearing his hair. In my time all the impresarios in Italy were bald at thirty.

I composed the overture to *Otello* in the Barbaja palace, wherein the baldest and fiercest of directors had forcibly locked me with a single plate of spaghetti and the threat that I would not be allowed to leave the room alive until I had written the last note.

I wrote the overture to *La Gazza Ladra* on the day of its opening in the theatre itself, where I was imprisoned by the director under the surveillance of four stagehands who were instructed to throw my manuscript out of the window, page by page, to the copyists waiting below to transcribe it. In default of pages, they were ordered to throw me out.

A commission to write a particular kind of work, for a particular occasion, or for particular performers can also be a great stimulus to creative activity. One need only think of Bach's cantatas, Haydn's symphonies, or Mozart's operas to realize that inspiration is not shy of the direct challenge. The mere fact that the music is wanted is an inspiration in itself.

The idea of composing music 'to order' was not popular in the nineteenth century. Composers then were inclined to think of themselves as men apart, bearers of some prophetic mission that must be fulfilled at all costs. Nowadays the older view has returned, and composers no longer think it slightly shameful to answer a specific request for music. Benjamin Britten's words would be echoed by most of his contemporaries:

When I am asked to compose a work for an occasion, great or small, I want to know in some detail the conditions of the place where it will be performed, the size and the acoustics, what instruments or singers will be available and suitable, the kind of people who will hear it, and what language they will understand—and even sometimes the age of the listeners and performers.

. . . such questions occupy one's attentions continuously, and certainly affect the stuff of music, and in my experience are not a restriction, but a challenge, an inspiration. Music does not exist in a vacuum, it does not exist until it is performed, and performance imposes conditions. It is the easiest thing in the world to write a piece virtually or totally impossible to perform—but oddly enough that is not what I prefer to do; I prefer to study the conditions of performance and shape my music to them.

This rather unromantic idea of the composer working to order may be easier to understand when it is realized that he does not have to be in the same mood as the music he wishes to create. To compose convincingly sad music he need not be plunged in deepest gloom, nor need he be especially merry in himself when he has to write something cheerful. For proof, we need think only of *The Magic Flute*, an opera filled with serene optimism and noble faith, written at a time when the conditions of Mozart's life were at their worst. Or of Beethoven, lonely and deaf, feeling his way to the sublime tranquillity of the last quartets.

Certainly, it is unlikely that a composer who had never known deep emotions would be able to express them in music. If he is to be a profound artist the composer must also be a man who has grown, through emotional experience. But when it comes to the moment of creation, what is needed is simply the ability to recall these emotions *in terms of music*. Tchaikovsky makes the point very clearly:

Those who imagine that a creative artist can, through the medium of his art, express his feelings at the moment when he is *moved*, make the greatest mistake. Emotions—sad or joyful—can only be expressed *retrospectively*, so to speak. Without any special reason for rejoicing I may be moved to the most cheerful creative mood; and vice versa, a work composed in the happiest surroundings may be touched with dark and gloomy colours.

In a word, the artist lives a double life: an everyday human life, and an artistic life; and the two do not always go hand in hand.

The truth of Tchaikovsky's remarks becomes quite evident when you consider how impossible it would be for a composer to remain in the same mood for the period of months it may take to complete a piece of music.

A cheerful mood may touch off musical invention as readily as a sad one. Composers are quite as able to express themselves when they are not crossed in love as when they are—though popular superstition prefers to have them with permanently broken hearts. The truth is that the composer is much more concerned with a job of work than the results of his labours may suggest. Neither he nor his music are at the mercy of his emotions, however much they may play their part.

5 · *Preliminaries to Composing*

EVEN the most gifted composer must study the basic grammar of his craft at some time in his career.

To begin with he must learn everything there is to know about musical notation. However clearly his music may sound in his head it will never exist for other people unless he can give precise instructions for playing it. Like the dramatist, the composer depends upon performers to interpret his ideas and make them a reality that everybody may enjoy.

Notation is best learned in learning to play an instrument. But the young composer must go a stage further than the average instrumentalist: he must learn how to hear the written symbols of notation as music, *in his head*.

However remarkable this accomplishment may appear to the layman, it can be learned like everything else. Just as a child must learn that certain letters make certain words, and that these have certain sounds and mean certain things, the composer learns an equivalent in music. It is all a question of training the memory. The young composer must fill his mind with remembered sounds—sounds that he will immediately associate with a correct notation. He must memorize also the sound of the different instruments, and the effect they make as they play together. All this can be done by listening carefully to music, while at the same time studying the printed score. It is no more mysterious a skill than any other.

Ideally, then, the young composer must sharpen his mind to the point where it can translate notation into imagined sound, and turn imagined (or real) sounds into notation. Once this has been achieved there is nothing to hinder the free flow of his invention—it can pass from mind to paper with the utmost speed.

Few young composers wait patiently until they have acquired these skills before attempting to compose. Indeed, the very act of struggling to put their ideas on paper helps them to learn what they need. And, as we have seen, it is quite permissible to turn to the piano, or any other instrument, to test the general effect of ideas before writing them down. Most composers regard the piano as an indispensable friend.

The composer of today has another friend: the tape-recorder. By recording a piano version of his score he can then sit back and judge its effect as a critical member of the audience might. He can see if its 'timing' is right—if it goes on a shade too long here, or is too perfunctory there, and if the overall shape seems balanced and convincing. Music is not just a matter of pretty tunes and beguiling harmonies: it is like a play, and occupies a space of time in which themes (the characters) must make their entries and exits at effective moments. Such matters are difficult to judge in the mind alone: imagined time need not be the same as clock time. Composers have even been known to revise an already printed score, after several hearings have convinced them that their first decisions were at fault. However annoying this may be for the publisher, these revisions speak highly for the nagging self-criticism that must be the composer's constant companion.

Music which is laid out to show, on separate lines, the part each instrument must play is said to be written in Full Score. The physical act involved in preparing such a score can be enormous. Each note must appear exactly in the right place and in a correct relationship with every other note. Dozens of signs must be added to show the manner in which the notes are to be played—whether soft or loud, fast or slow, smoothly or spikily. In the two bars that make up the first page of Vaughan Williams's Sixth Symphony (p. 36) there are some three hundred notes, and a great many modifying signs and directions. Yet these two bars take only five seconds to perform—five seconds out of a work that lasts thirty-four minutes! Writing a full score is certainly no easy matter.

Despite the complexity of modern musical notation, composers mostly agree that it is an inadequate way of showing the finer points of what they have imagined. There is always some subtlety that cannot be expressed in writing, always something that must be left to the performer's imagination. And it can easily happen that the performer fails to grasp the composer's intention, and so passes on an insensitive and inadequate account of the music.

Only composers of electronic music have complete control over the performance of their works. Here the very act of creation fixes the performance once and for all: the composer is his own interpreter.

Although the equipment and methods involved in producing electronic music may seem strange, the process

To Michael Mullinar

SYMPHONY IN E MINOR

I   ALLEGRO

R. VAUGHAN WILLIAMS

Orchestral Score and Parts may be hired from the Publishers

Copyright, 1948, by the Oxford University Press, London

Printed in Great Britain.

itself is as much a creative act as orthodox methods of composition. The trappings may be those of the physics laboratory—wave generators, oscillators and the like; the recording studio—tape recorders, loudspeakers and amplifiers; and the mathematician—frequency ratios and stopwatch timings; but the mind that controls them must be served by a sensitive ear and a musical imagination.

For those who value the 'human' quality in music, however, this is not a satisfactory state of affairs. Even the finest performance can grow stale upon repetition—as any gramophone record will prove. No two live performances are ever alike. The minute variations in each interpretation have a value of their own: the music is in a constant state of re-creation, and each performance brings a new dimension to the composer's original vision.

It is for this reason that many composers are wary not only of electronic music, but also of any attempt to make musical notation more complicated. The more control the composer has over interpretation, the more the performer is reduced to the level of a machine making an automatic and always identical response. Most composers are therefore content to risk the occasional disaster.

Certain *avant-garde* composers have even made a virtue out of the element of chance that must accompany all live performances. Often abandoning conventional forms of notation, they provide their interpreters with a chart of symbols designed to stimulate an imaginative musical response. Precisely what that response is to be is left to the performer, who creates the work as he goes along. No two performances are ever alike, and rehearsals take on another meaning.

Sometimes actual notation is provided, but opportunities

are then left for the performer to decide the final pattern. Such directions as 'play the movements in any order', 'begin on any note' are frequent. The aim is to involve the composer, performer, and listener in a spontaneous creative experience, offered not necessarily as a musical composition in the traditional sense, but as a spirited form of music-making. The usual term applied to these processes is *aleatory*, and certain oriental philosophies are invoked as their justification.

On the opposite page is a sample of *avant-garde* notation, from 'Siciliano' by Sylvano Bussotti.

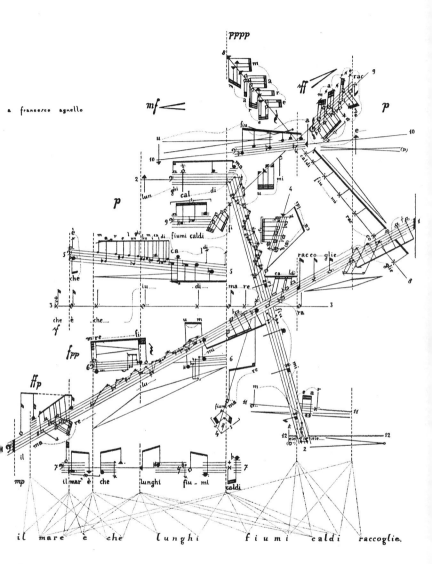

Bussotti "Siciliano" © Edizioni Bruzzichelli

6 · *The Student Composer*

THERE is no one way of teaching the art of composition. There are even strong reasons for saying that it cannot be taught at all, and that each young composer must simply teach himself by trial and error. And certainly composers who have been entirely self-taught, like Elgar, have produced work every bit as good as those who, like Vaughan Williams, have studied assiduously at musical training centres and submitted themselves to official examination.

The problems involved in trying to teach composition spring from one fact: in art, theory must follow practice. Rules are derived from the careful study of what has been done in the past. As the art changes, so new rules suggest themselves. It is therefore extremely difficult to teach the latest advances in any art. The ground is not sufficiently tested for guiding rules to have emerged, and the would-be teacher may know very little more than his pupil. In this area particularly the young composer must teach himself; and he does this, as we have seen, by imitating the music he most admires.

But it is unlikely that a student-composer will make much headway with modern methods unless he has some kind of yardstick to measure them by. That yardstick can only be supplied by the study of what composers have done in the past, and it is here that academic rules and regulations become valuable.

Nowadays most academies divide the composer's preparatory studies into: harmony, counterpoint, musical form, and orchestration. This is a mere convenience: all, of course, are blended in the act of composition.

By the study of harmony the student learns how to move convincingly from one chord to another. From counterpoint he learns how to combine independent melodies. By studying form he learns how music can be given an effective external shape. And by the study of orchestration he learns what the different instruments can do, by themselves and in combination.

Most studies in harmony and counterpoint concentrate on the example of two historical periods: the mainly contrapuntal sixteenth century (Palestrina and his contemporaries), and the harmonically inclined eighteenth century (Bach to Beethoven). These periods are chosen because they represent two fairly stable moments in musical development, from which it is therefore easy to draw definite rules of conduct. The young composer learns how to imitate the style of these periods, and thus gains an insight into the way great masters have put their music together. At the same time he is trained in a method of approach that will help him when he comes to study the music of other periods.

The value of academic exercises also lies in the discipline they impose on the mind. They force the composer to manipulate the materials of music according to certain generally accepted rules. The more he learns how to overcome the difficulties, the more skilful he becomes as a composer. In a very literal sense he 'exercises' his musical technique, just as an athlete will train his body.

Academic study need not, of course, be restricted to the music of the past. Certain modern techniques—notably those of serial music—proceed along well-defined lines and can thus be taught with some confidence.

All the academic study in the world, however, will not turn a man into a composer unless he has an inborn talent for composition. But it is equally true that the gifted man cannot fail to improve his talents by study. Nobody pretends that the mature composer will not shake off academic restraint and begin to create, through his originality, rules of his own. But before he can do this with confidence, he must first have proved himself the master of his materials.

There have been few composers who have not believed in the need for formal studies. Even the most revolutionary —the Beethovens and the Schoenbergs—have made their own pupils undergo a rigorous training in traditional techniques. However much they may have broken the rules as composers, they have believed in them as teachers.

Besides perfecting his technique through exercises, the young composer will, of course, write music of his own. His teacher will cast an experienced eye over this, pointing out where the music seems to take a wrong turn or fails to make the best use of its material. Together they will examine the music of other men, to discover how they have

Opposite, a page from a famous guide to composers and others, Thomas Morley's *A Plaine and Easie Introduction to Musicke* (1595). The teacher berates the pupil for over-confidence.

Phi. I thinke it shal be no hard matter for me to imitate this.

Ma. Set downe your waie, and then I wil tel you how wel you haue don it.

Phi. Here it is, and I thinke it shall need but little correction.

Ma. Conceit of their own sufficiencie hath o-uerthrowne many, who otherwise woulde haue proued excellent. There fore in anie case, neuer thinke so well of your

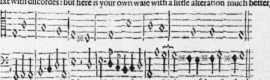

selfe but let, other men praise you, if you bee praise worthie : then may you iustlie take it to your selfe, so it bee done with moderation and without arrogancie.

Phi. I will: but wherein doe you condemne my waie?

Ma. In those thinges wherein I did not thinke you should haue erred. For in the be-ginning of your fourth note, you take a discord for the first part, & not in binding wise: your other faults are not so grosse, and yet must they be told.

A discord take for the first part of a note not in binding wise cōdemned

Phi. In what notes be they?

Ma. In the foure notes going before the close, for there your descant woulde haue beene more stirring, and by reason it hangs so much, I do not, nor cannot greatly com-mend it, although it be true in the cordes.

Phi. What? Is not that binding descant good?

Ma. That kind of binding with concords is not so good as those bindinges which are mixt with discordes: but here is your own waie with a little alteration much better.

binding with concords not so good as that with discords.

Phi. This is the course of the world, that where we thinke our selues surest, there are we furthest off from our purpose. And I thought verilie, that if there could haue beene anie fault found in my waie, it should haue bin so final, that it should not haue bin worth the speaking of. But when we haue a little, we straight imagine that wee haue all, when God knowes the least part of that which we know not, is more then al we know. There-fore I praie you yet set me another example, that considering it with your other, I may more cleerelie perceiue the artificiall composition of them both.

Ma. Here be two, choose which of them you thinke best and imitate it.

N

tackled similar problems. The teacher may very well suggest that his pupil should write different kinds of music—for example, if he delights in writing piano pieces, clotted with handfuls of notes and thick, luscious chords, he would certainly benefit from being made to write for string quartet.

In short: the true teacher stands as guardian to the young composer's budding sense of self-criticism. If he can awaken this into a full and active life he will have done his duty, the rest he can safely leave to the composer himself.

Radiophonic studio at the BBC, used (among other things) for composing electronic music – see page 37.

7 · The Sources of Income

THE composer of today earns his living in ways that are quite different from those open to composers of the past. If he is unlucky he may still, of course, starve. But, given a reasonable degree of luck, and talent, and common sense, he can expect a greater reward for his labours than ever before. The composer who dies a wealthy man is a distinctly twentieth-century invention.

Until about the year 1800 the vast majority of composers were employed as servants, either of the church or some wealthy nobleman. Like Bach, they were organists and choirmasters: teaching their choristers, playing for church services, and writing whatever music was needed for the daily life of the church. Like Haydn, they were in charge of music at some court: training and conducting the orchestra, preparing music for the private chapel and opera house, and, again, writing music for every occasion.

For these services they were paid a living wage, and enjoyed the occasional extra mark of favour—the winter's firewood, perhaps, or a gold snuff-box from some visiting dignitary. They were servants (Haydn, for example, wore court livery like any footman) but they were not slaves. The work they did was, for the most part, appreciated and actually wanted by the people who employed them. Their music did not gather dust on the shelves for want of a performance. They had a definite place in society.

This kind of composing life only began to change when music started to reach out to a paying audience: first through the opera house, after about 1650, and then through the rise of public concerts a hundred years later. By the end of the eighteenth century the change was nearly complete. Composers thereafter began to demand the right to work on their own terms, and compose as they thought fit. A grateful world ought to be glad to pay for the privilege of being offered a masterpiece.

Looked at quite coldly and without any sentimentality about 'the burning mission of the great artist', the move towards independence had its dangers. At its noblest it could lead to virtual self-sacrifice on the part of the artist for the sake of a deeply-held belief in the value of his work. But it could also lead to the kind of arrogance that says 'I alone know what is good for you. I shall force my work on you, and then complain bitterly if you do not accept it without question'. Wagner's extraordinary career provides examples of both kinds of attitude.

As the nineteenth century wore on, concerts became more and more profitable and the publication of music began to develop into a major industry. Composers, however, were a little late in establishing a legal right to a fair share in the money that was now to be made. For a long time no one had to pay to perform their music, and anyone could steal it. And it was only gradually that a code of behaviour grew up between composers, publishers, and performers. International agreements were eventually set up to safeguard the rights of anyone who had any claim to own music.

Even today few composers earn their living entirely by composing. Though a handful may earn very large sums indeed (composers of popular music, like Richard Rodgers, or serious composers with an international reputation, like Stravinsky or Benjamin Britten), the vast majority are obliged to do some other musical job to make ends meet. More often than not they teach, either privately or at some musical academy or school. A few work for publishers, and some for radio and television companies. A very few are in demand as performers. Others, we may suppose, wash dishes or live on charity.

The income to be had directly from composing derives from the fact that the composer is said, by most civilized countries, to own his work from the moment it is committed to paper. He controls the *copyright* in his work and is therefore entitled to be paid for public performances, publication, recordings, and so on. This copyright remains with him until he dies, and then passes to his heirs for a period of fifty years. Thereafter the work becomes public property and may be freely used by anyone.

It is very much to the composer's advantage to have a publisher who, in return for a share in the copyright, will print his music, advertise it, and generally help to bring about performances. With an alert publisher behind him, the composer can then get on with his music, happy in the knowledge that his best interests are now being looked after.

A composer's income comes from a number of sources. First, there is the royalty paid by the publisher on the sale of each piece of music. This is usually ten per cent of the published price. A piece of music selling at five shillings will therefore earn sixpence for its composer every time a

copy is sold. This may seem as if the publisher is taking the lion's share of the profits, but, as we shall see in the next chapter, the costs of publishing and printing make it impossible to offer the composer better terms. The arrangement, in fact, is quite fair.

Compared with fifty years ago, very little printed music is sold nowadays and the composer cannot expect royalties to provide much of an income. This decline is due mainly to the invention of broadcasting and gramophone records, both of which tend to discourage people from making music in their own homes. As we shall see, however, record companies and broadcasting stations pay for the use of copyright music and, at least in the case of the most popular composers, this more than makes up for any loss.

Anyone who borrows orchestral parts and scores from the publisher pays a hiring fee. The composer gets anything from a quarter to half of this. The actual hiring fees vary according to the nature of the work, and are different for amateur and professional performances. One performance of a thirty-minute work might bring in twelve or fifteen guineas from a professional orchestra, and five from amateurs.

Of much greater importance, to composer and publisher alike, are 'performing fees'. A concert hall, or any other place where music is performed in public, must pay an annual fee to the Performing Right Society. It is then obliged by law to make regular returns to the Society,

Opposite, humans and machines at work for the Performing Right Society.

49

listing everything that has been performed within its walls. The Society calculates how many minutes of each composer's music has been played during the year, and then forwards him a proportion of the total licence fees. Thus, a composer who has had one hundred minutes' music performed will get more than a composer who has only had twenty minutes. 'Serious' music is paid on a higher scale than 'pop'—but 'pop', of course, commands many more minutes of performance.

The money paid out during the course of a year to individual composers varies enormously. A few shillings at one end of the scale, and so on, up to perhaps twenty-five thousand pounds in the case of the most popular composers. The vast majority, however, can reckon their earnings in tens and hundreds of pounds.

The P.R.S. licensing system operates wherever music is performed—in public houses, bingo halls, youth clubs, factories, as well as concert halls. The licence fees are often very small, and are always based on the circumstances of performance. Music at a Flower Show, for example, would be licensed at a fee of two or three shillings. On the other hand, the annual block fees paid out by such bodies as the B.B.C. are very considerable and can account for a very large part of the average composer's earnings.

Theatrical music—opera, ballet, incidental music for plays, and so forth—comes under a different heading. Here, individual terms are arranged: sometimes, as in opera or ballet, a percentage of the box-office takings, divided between the composer and his publisher; sometimes, as with incidental music, a flat fee, which will vary according to the reputation of the composer and the amount of work involved.

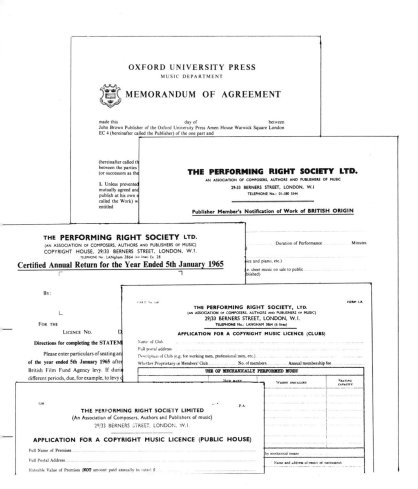

The royalties paid by gramophone record companies also come under a separate heading. They are known as Mechanical Rights, and in England usually amount to six and a quarter per cent of the retail price of the record (not counting Purchase Tax, of course). Publisher and composer normally split this royalty on a fifty-fifty basis. The fact that Mechanical Rights are the only royalties fixed by law, and therefore not open to negotiation, and are in any case very small indeed, make them a source of irritation to composers and publishers—though not, of course, to record companies. Even so, they can bring in very useful sums of money to the popular composer.

All these schemes operate internationally. A composer may expect a fee even if his music is being performed or recorded in a country he has never heard of. Only a very few countries (among them the Soviet Union) do not belong to the movement.

These, then, are the direct ways in which the composer's music can earn him a living. But there are other sources of income that are equally important.

High on the list comes the writing of music for films. Not every composer can face the exacting requirements of this medium, but, for those who can, the rewards are considerable. In England, a composer of standing in the film world (he may not necessarily be a composer of standing in the musical world) can expect anything from one thousand to two thousand pounds for work on a large scale film, and will also, of course, receive performing right fees whenever the film is shown. Thirty minutes of music in a successful film can bring in a very handsome sum over the years. Cynical composers say that the worse the film is the more you are likely to earn.

Of rising importance are the various forms of direct patronage. The composer may be asked to write a work for a particular occasion and be offered a fee for the right of first performance. The patron may be a private individual, the committee of a music festival, a radio company, an opera house, the directors of a large business concern (anxious to improve the company's image by giving money to the arts), a church, a school—anyone you care to mention. The fee too may be anything—from ten pounds for a church anthem, to five hundred for a symphony, or a thousand for an opera. Everything depends on the occasion, the importance of the composer, and how much money there is to spend.

In the same way, radio and television companies often commission special music for their dramatic productions. Each company has its own scale of payment and, as it were, buys the music 'by the minute'.

Sometimes a large publishing house will offer the composer a small regular income for the right to handle all his music. This is known as a retaining fee—a 'retainer'. The composer's royalties are still paid in the normal way, and there is no question of his being asked to repay the retainer at a later date. Such sums vary very much in size, from perhaps a hundred pounds upwards. At least one of a thousand pounds has been known in this country, but it is quite exceptionally large. This kind of patronage is particularly helpful to the young composer, for it not only increases his confidence, but also buys him the time that is needed to produce the kind of works that will bring credit to himself and his publisher.

Of rather less importance—simply because, in England at least, they are so few and far between—are the various prizes, awards, and fellowships on offer to composers. The prize may come out of the blue from some discerning patron, or it may be competed for in connection with some public event. Fellowships are offered by universities—some even like to harbour their own 'resident composer', who is expected to show his gratitude by teaching a little and composing a great deal.

Only in Soviet Russia does the composer come under the direct patronage, and control, of the State. He is cared for and rewarded handsomely. He composes for the State and is published by it. He is performed and may even become internationally famous. But he must be careful not to give offence. Few Western composers consider that, on balance, the arrangement is worth imitating.

8 · *The Music Publisher*

ALTHOUGH the business of printing and selling music started over four hundred years ago, music publishing as we know it today only began to get into its stride towards the end of the eighteenth century. It was the courage and enterprise shown by the English firm of Novello during the first half of the nineteenth century that really turned music publishing into big business.

Alfred Novello took the risk of printing music in large quantities and then selling it at prices that ordinary music-lovers could afford. He was the first publisher ever to do this, and despite the gloomy prophecies of wiser heads his action succeeded. Choral music, his main stand-by, sold in enormous quantities. He was soon able to bring his prices down still further and, in consequence, sold more. Other publishing houses were forced to follow his example and thus the whole pattern of music publishing entered a new and exciting phase. It is only in recent years that conditions are again having to be rethought.

The history of music, of course, has been and is still being enlivened by the cries of composers raging against their publishers. But, on the whole, the partnership has been smooth and to their mutual advantage. If there have been occasions when a publisher has exploited a composer mercilessly, there have also been moments when composers have played dubious tricks. The warfare has never been wholly one-sided.

Composers find it very easy to forget that music publishing is a business which, like all businesses, must show a profit if it is to survive. Each piece of music published represents an act of faith on the part of the publisher. He backs his judgement. If that judgement is sound he makes a profit, and so does the composer. If not, the loss is his alone.

The wise publisher does not expect an immediate return on the money he invests. Often it may be years before any kind of balance is struck, let alone a profit made. During such times the unprofitable composer is, so to speak, subsidized by his more successful colleagues. Later, with luck, his music will begin to bring in money that can be used to launch younger composers.

Each publisher will try to find some stable, profitable line of business to provide the bread and butter of his working capital. He may specialize in editions of the popular classics, or in educational music. He may do something altogether different from music publishing—as in the case of Boosey & Hawkes, who make musical instruments, and Novellos, who are printers in their own right. The steady income from such ventures pays for the day-to-day running costs and enables the publisher to take risks on unknown quantities—the 'prestige' composer whose cause he helps to fight.

And make no mistake about it: the running costs of a large, modern publishing house are enormous.

It is not just a matter of having the music printed (few publishers actually print their own). New works must be advertised and promoted in the face of keen competition. A dispatch department must be ready to send copies to any part of the world. The accounts department must be ready with balanced books, and cheques for the composer whose music has earned its keep. There must be 'readers' to decide whether the flood of manuscripts contains anything worth publishing. Secretaries, salesmen, cleaners and office-boys—all the paraphernalia of the modern business world, in fact. Merely to keep this vast organization ticking over calls for enormous reserves of capital.

What happens when a manuscript arrives at the publisher's office? Obviously, if it is the work of an established, important composer the procedure is automatic: it is prepared for publication as soon as possible. Nine times out of ten the composer will already have warned his publisher that a new work is on the way, and may even have consulted him about its details. The publisher may, in fact, have been responsible for the work being written in the first place, by arranging a commission, or a first performance. The odds are that the publisher will work with an important composer on the closest terms through all the stages of composition; and then, when the manuscript arrives, everything will be ready and waiting to bring it before the public.

With composers who are well known, but not famous, the procedure is a little different. Even if the new work is good, the publisher must consider very carefully whether it represents a reasonable business risk. If, for example, it happens to be a sonata for violin and piano and he has just published three such works by other men, the publisher can hardly be expected to feel much enthusiasm. There is no point in flooding the market with works that will only have to compete against each other.

Music from an unknown composer will be examined very carefully indeed. Of the manuscripts that come thudding on to the publisher's desk in daily streams, by far the greater number are worthless. An expert eye can sort these out in a matter of minutes and they are returned with a polite rejection slip. The publisher does not enter into correspondence over his reasons for turning a work down—life is too short, postage too heavy, and libel actions can be brought too easily.

A composer's manuscript.

The short list of 'possibles' is then examined in detail. The lucky work is accepted and the composer informed and offered a contract. And who knows if it may not be the beginning of a long and mutually profitable association?

The publisher has many reasons for rejecting even a work which he knows to have musical value. He may not be interested in that particular kind of music—all publishers have their pet fields. He may, as we have seen, be already top-heavy with similar work. He may reluctantly have to admit that there is simply no market for this kind of music, however good: imagine, for example, how many people are interested in song-cycles, or chamber music. And he may have accepted so much already that he dare not take any more for fear of falling behind on his publishing schedule. The composer who has measured his own worth from a truly critical standpoint need never be dismayed and discouraged by a rejection slip.

Before a manuscript is sent to the printer it must be carefully checked by the publisher's editor. This is not merely to guard against possible slips of the pen, but to ensure that every detail conforms to the publisher's 'house style'. The manuscript must be a handwritten version of what the printed music will be like.

Some composers are very slapdash in the way they put their music on paper. This will not do for the printer. For him every mark must be in exactly the right place, and every aspect of the score must tell a consistent tale. Musical notation is not the sound of music, but a series of directions to the performer telling him how that sound may be produced. Any vagueness or ambiguity can only lead to disaster.

Before the manuscript goes to the printer the publisher

will make a detailed estimate of the printing costs. The size and nature of the work, the format in which it will appear, the number of copies to be printed, and many other factors will enter into his calculations. Indeed, this estimate can play an important part in the publisher's decision to accept a work in the first place.

When all these points have been settled the manuscript is sent to the printer. In the next chapter we shall consider how printed music is produced. Here we may simply note that before the final printing takes place a rough copy is sent to the composer so that he can check that no errors have crept in, and that everything is just as he intended. This rough copy is known as a *proof*. In passing it the composer accepts the final responsibility for the printed music.

The proof is also checked by members of the publisher's staff, for it is astonishing how easy it is for small errors to pass unobserved—the dot missed from a dotted crotchet, for example. It is then returned to the printer, who makes good the mistakes and then completes the printing.

Exactly how many copies are run off at the first printing depends very much on the kind of music and the importance of the composer. Obviously, a new work by William Walton or Benjamin Britten is of greater interest to the musical world than the first publication of an unknown composer, and consequently can be expected to sell more copies. But, in very general terms, the publisher always hopes that the first print will cover the basic costs of production. Further printings, which cost less to produce, will then attend to the profits.

Deciding what price to sell the music at can be very difficult. It is not simply a matter of dividing production costs by the number of copies printed. The publisher must

A corrected proof, ready to go back to the printer.

also take into account his firm's 'overheads'—the day-to-day running costs. Different firms calculate in different ways, but, as a general rule of thumb, most of them arrive at a *trade* price (the price the music trade pays, as opposed to the *retail* price, which is what the public pays), by doubling the production costs, adding in the composer's royalty (calculated on the retail price, of course) and then rounding up.

For example: it would cost about £150 to print two thousand copies of a twenty-page vocal score. Each copy therefore costs 1s. 6d. to produce. To strike the economic price, the publisher doubles this, adds in the composer's royalty (about 6d.) and thus arrives at a minimum trade price of 3s. 6d. He may very well decide that a more reasonable trade price is 4s.; and then the trade adds on its own profit allowance (twenty per cent in the case of vocal music) and the public finally buys the music at 5s. a copy.

On the face of it, this looks as if the publisher allows himself a very generous profit margin. But in fact he will be lucky if the first printing does anything more than clear his total expenses. And a lot of music never reaches a reprint.

There are also some pieces of music which have to be sold at an absolutely uneconomic price—simply because the true price would be beyond the average music-lover's pocket. For example: a 100-page study score of a symphony might cost £600 to produce. If the composer is very important the initial print will be of a thousand copies. Half these may go in the first year, but the rest will settle down to sell at a steady fifty a year, or thereabouts. The first print will therefore take about ten years to sell out. If the composer is not so well known only five hundred copies will be run off. On the five hundred copy basis the cost of each score would be 24s., and this would imply a final retail price of four guineas. The most any publisher could dare suggest for such a work would be two guineas, and so he is bound to make a loss. And even with the work of the important composer he will have to wait many years before he sees his money back. The publisher will only involve himself in such undertakings if he thinks that performing and hire fees may help to balance the books. He prints the score partly as a gesture of good-will, and partly as a means of advertising the music.

It goes without saying that a really large-scale work, like an opera, which may cost six or seven thousand pounds to print, usually amounts to little more than an impressive way of losing money.

If a publisher wishes to handle a work, but cannot see his way clear to print it, he can place it in his Hire Library. This consists of manuscript copies of scores and orchestral parts, neatly made by professional copyists and ready to be hired out at an appropriate fee. Should the demand suddenly become overwhelming, new copies can easily be made by photography. Nearly all orchestral parts, even those of highly successful works, exist in this form. It is simply not worth the publisher's while to have them printed.

The Hire Library system also imposes a very useful check on the number of performances that can slip by without anyone paying for the privilege of using the music. It is still quite easy to buy a few copies of a piece of music, give a performance and do nothing about licence fees or anything else. The odds are that the publisher will never know—or only find out when it is too late to do anything —and even the Performing Right Society's watchdogs cannot be everywhere at once. When the music is hired the publisher at least knows that a performance is in the offing.

Once the printed, or copied music is ready, the business of promoting and advertising it begins. The composer receives a number of free copies for his own use, and so do a great many other people. A copy of a new clarinet sonata, for example, will be sent to each of the most prominent clarinet soloists and teachers. Choral works will be placed with the organizers of appropriate festivals and the conductors of such choirs as have been interested in similar works. The publisher's salesmen will take copies of new works to music shops round the country, and to schools and training colleges when they make their regular visits. Copies will be sent to magazines with a respectful request for 'the favour of a review'. In short, everything will be done to bring the new music to the attention of the musical world.

And if the musical world responds by buying the music and performing it, then all is well. The publisher will see his money back. The composer will receive welcome cheques and, doubtless, requests for more music. And the printer will be told to prepare a further impression.

9 · *Printing the Music*

CONSIDER the page in front of you. In setting it up, the printer has had a number of points to bear in mind. Each line must be perfectly horizontal and begin and end at exactly the same place down the margins. Each word must be suitably spaced inside its line, so that the eye does not run one into another. Each letter in the word must be equally spaced from the next—a sudden gap and the word will break in two. Spelling and punctuation must be accurate.

These are problems enough. But they are nothing to the task that faces the printer of a musical score.

Music must be read vertically as well as horizontally. The notes of each instrumental part must not only be accurate in themselves, but also appear in an exact relationship with the notes of every other part in the score. In the same space of time one instrument may have a dozen notes to play, another two, another five, and so on through an infinity of combinations. The precise relationships must be immediately apparent to the eye.

Add to this the problem of coping with notes that leap from top to bottom of the stave; the problem of leaving space for playing directions, or words for the voices to sing; and the overall problem of laying out each bar so that the notes are grouped in a way that immediately suggests their relationships, and you will see that the printer's task is not an easy one.

Consider also how necessary it is for him to be absolutely accurate. If the word 'awey' suddenly appears in a book, the reader will read 'away' and ignore the obvious error. But displace a note by the merest fraction—print B instead of A—and a totally different sound will float out, to everyone's embarrassment.

If you examine the book you are now reading, you will find that here and there the printer has had to divide a word that will not fit neatly into its line. A hyphen joins the two halves and all is well. Nor has it mattered if the last few words in a paragraph fall short of a complete line. A blank is left, and the effect is perfectly acceptable. The paragraph does not even have to fit into the page—it can start at the bottom of one and finish at the top of the next. And it makes not the slightest difference if the last page of a chapter consists merely of a few words and an ocean of blank paper.

The music printer has no such licence. He cannot have half a bar on one page and the remainder on the turn-over. He must space out his bars so that they fit the page snugly and inevitably. He would consider his work amateurish in the extreme if the last page had to be left half empty. In short: he *designs* each page with the utmost care.

Music printing began at the end of the fifteenth century. Notes and staves were carved out of a single wooden block: the marks on the paper being the raised part of the wood carving, and the white spaces the gaps where the wood had been chipped away. The result was rather clumsy.

The next solution involved setting up individual pieces of music-type: a jigsaw puzzle of hundreds of bits of metal. Again it was a laborious process, but it survived for certain kinds of music (notably, hymn tunes) until recent times.

An example of music set by movable type.

Even in the best examples, however, slight irregularities, hair-cracks and minute deviations from the horizontal and vertical can be detected.

The beginning of the seventeenth century saw the introduction of engraved metal plates. In this process the music is cut into thin sheets of copper or pewter. The lines are then filled with a sticky ink, which can be transferred to sheets of paper pressed against the plate.

A fourth method, *lithography*, was invented in 1796 by a German actor and dramatist, Alois Senefelder.

Senefelder discovered that a certain kind of stone found in Bavaria had a natural affinity for grease, absorbed water, and reacted variously to chemicals. He took flat, dry, polished stones of this kind and wrote music on them in a special greasy ink. This sank into the stone in firm, clear lines. He then covered the surface with a thin film of water, which, of course, settled everywhere but where the greasy lines were drawn. Next, he rolled the moist stone with ink. This stuck only to the original greasy marks in the stone and would not settle where the moisture lay. Thus, when he pressed a piece of paper against the stone it took up the ink that the greasy marks had attracted and gave him his printed copy. By repeating the process of damping and inking he was able to take dozens of copies from the same stone. It was necessary, of course, to write backwards on the stone in the first place (from right to left) in order to have the music appear the right way round on the paper.

The stones, however, were heavy and cracked easily, and in 1805 he discovered a method of using metal plates in their stead. This process, known as *metal-plate lithography*, became the basis of all music printing. It is still used today, but is now linked with engraving and photography, which are made to lead up to it.

Engraving is a highly specialized art. It is also a dying art, for it is very expensive and new methods have had to be found to take its place. In a few years it may very well have vanished altogether. Nevertheless, its basic principles are worth considering.

In each workshop there is a Foreman Engraver, who is

An engraver at work.

responsible for solving all the problems of lay-out mentioned earlier in the chapter. When he has made his calculations he takes a soft-metal plate and marks out roughly where each stave, each bar line, each note and each word will appear. He passes this to the engravers, who begin by cutting in the staves with a five-point graver. Then, using a series of steel punches, each with the appropriate symbols raised up on one end, they add the words (if any) and the note heads.

The engravers stamp these marks into the metal, lightly tapping the punches with a small hammer. They then take different shapes and sizes of steel gravers (short blades mounted on bulbous wooden handles that fit the palm) and cut in the stems and tails of the notes, the phrase-marks and slurs. This they do entirely free-hand, drawing in a firm straight line or a gently swelling curve with unerring skill. Thus: all the fixed symbols, from note-heads to treble clefs, are stamped in with punches; and all the variable symbols are cut in with gravers. And everything is done backwards, from right to left in mirror fashion. On average, it takes about three hours to complete each plate.

When all the plates are complete, a proof is pulled. The plates are rolled with sticky green ink, which clings to the flat surface but does not dribble into the engraved cavities. A sheet of paper is pressed against this, takes up the ink, and shows the notes and lines in white against a green background. This proof is sent to the composer for checking. Errors in the engraving can be made good by tapping the metal back into place from behind (the plate is turned over) and recutting the surface. Once the proofs have been passed, the plates are ready for the next stage in the printing process.

In order to make use of modern high-speed methods of printing, the contents of each engraved plate must now be transferred to a large sheet of zinc—the first step in an ingenious adaption of the old lithographic process, known as *photo-lithography*.

The zinc sheet must be thought of as the equivalent of Senefelder's stone. In order to make it hold a thin film of water, as the stone did through its natural properties, the zinc plate is *grained*—that is: given a slightly rough surface, so that the water will sit in millions of tiny cavities. The grained plate is then coated with bichromated albumen

Printing by offset photo lithography.

and becomes, to all intents and purposes, a photographic plate. The special property of this coating is that it will harden when exposed to light, but otherwise can be washed off in water.

It is now necessary to make a 'negative' from the engraved plate. This is taken in exactly the same way as the proof—only now the background is jet black, with the music in white. The negative is placed on the sensitive zinc plate and locked in a vacuum printing frame. Arc lamps are switched on. The light passes through the white parts of the negative and hardens the surface beneath. The black parts hold back the light and the sensitive surface beneath then remains soluble.

Immediately after exposure the zinc plate is rolled with greasy ink and then developed in water. The soluble parts wash away, together with the ink on them, and the hardened parts remain, complete with a film of greasy ink. The zinc plate is now in the condition of Senefelder's prepared stone. It is fitted to the revolving cylinder of a litho printing press, which carries out all the stages of damping and inking described earlier, and so the music is printed.

Rather less than half the music printed today makes use of the engraved plate, photo–litho sequence. The rest employs photo–lithography, but finds a cheaper substitute for the engraved plate. Several methods are used, and new ones seem to be invented each year. They remain more or less the secret of their owners. But they have one thing in common: they can all be carried out by comparatively unskilled labour—which is more than can be said for engraving.

Indeed, this is a time of change for the whole of the music printing industry. The recent invention of a practical music typewriter may well lead to new methods. And already the development of purely photographic reproduction has led to a revival of the copyist's art.

Most orchestral full-scores are now photographed direct from a hand-written copy. If the composer's manuscript is sufficiently legible it can be photographed direct. More often, however, a special copy is made by a professional copyist who has developed clear, elegant writing to a fine art. Usually he writes on a semi-transparent manuscript paper, in solid black ink. This is then placed in a photographic machine, together with a piece of sensitized paper which turns first into a negative (white note against a yellow background) and then into a positive (black notes on white paper) all in a matter of seconds.

Amazing results can be obtained from hand-copying, but it is not a cheap process. First-rate copyists are as rare as first-rate engravers, and are therefore paid well. Nor is it necessarily a quick method. In a really complicated modern score it may take a hard day's work to complete even one page. Whichever way you go about it, reproducing a composer's score is an expensive business.

Once printed, the music is cut by machine into appropriate pages and gathered together like a book, ready to be bound or stapled into its covers. The printer notifies the publisher, who takes the copies into his warehouse and announces publication.

10 · *The First Performance*

DELIGHTED as most composers are to see their music in print, publication is not the goal they have been working towards. Far more important are performances, and in particular the first performance. This is the moment that really matters to the composer—the moment when his score is translated into sound, and that sound is communicated to other men and women for the first time.

The composer's attitude to the first performance is almost invariably mixed. He is eager to see if his ideas will be understood and accepted, and yet he is fearful that something will go wrong and bring about a completely false impression of what he was trying to say. However old a hand he is at the game, the experience is nerveracking.

Most sensible musicians confronted with a new work will, if it is at all possible, consult the composer himself. This is simply a wise precaution, because, as we have seen, musical notation cannot be an absolutely precise account of the composer's intentions, however careful he may have been. There is always something that must be left to the interpreter's sympathetic understanding. Far better, then, to try out various shades of interpretation on the composer himself before appearing in public.

Such consultations can be a great help to the composer, and he will welcome them. He may, as a result, decide to make slight alterations, especially if the score hasn't actually been printed and the performance is being given from manuscript or photographed copies. No composer worth his salt objects to making changes, providing, of course, they are sensible and practical and do not damage the main line of his musical thought. Indeed, it is generally found that the greater the composer the more ready he is to take advice. The point at issue is the need for a thoroughly effective performance, and not the infallibility of his genius.

Very early in every composer's career there comes the realization that no performance, however good, can ever quite match the private performance that went on in his head as he wrote the work. For this, after all, took place in the perfect concert hall, and was given by a band of archangels before an audience of angels. The frailties of human existence never came into it.

In real life no two performances will ever be the same. Even if they are both good, they will be good in different ways. Each time a piece of music is played it must be re-created by the performers. To the composer this is both a source of delight and misery: delight when he hears his work unfold in a telling way; misery when things go wrong.

And dozens of things can go wrong in even the best regulated performances. Horns can crack a note, strings slip out of tune, singers can suddenly lose voice. Audiences may break out in an epidemic of coughing, or, worse still, shuffling and whispering. The concert hall may be too hot, or too cold, or half empty. The programme may have been miscalculated, so that the new work is overshadowed or in some way prejudiced by the other pieces. Indeed, it is a miracle that things so often go right.

Bearing this in mind, it is easy to see why composers do not much enjoy having their music judged on the strength of one performance. However thorough the rehearsals may have been, and however good the performance may seem, a new work will never have had time to sink into the performer's subconscious in the way that an old classic will have done. The interpretation is bound to be raw and tentative.

In the same way, no audience can absorb and understand a new work on one hearing—nor indeed can a music critic. But such is the fascination of the words 'first performance' that music-lovers flock to attend them, and they are bread and butter to the critics.

Ideally, no music should be burdened with this kind of irrelevant publicity. Rather, it should appear and be accepted or rejected and go on its way from there. The time to judge it comes later. The musical world, however, prefers the excitement of the 'first' performance. Presumably audiences hope they may be lucky enough to attend what later proves to have been an historic event—something they can tell their children about. But, from the composer's point of view, the hundredth performance would be much more an occasion for rejoicing. Even a second performance is more significant—for, as every composer will tell you, these are often the most difficult to obtain!

People often think that the composer must be in a state of ecstasy as he listens to a performance of his music. The odds are that he is not. The most trivial mishap will wound him deeply. He will be morbidly aware of the work's shortcomings—no need for the critic to tell him in to-

A composer at rehearsal. Sir William Walton, o.m.

morrow's papers. He may even learn things about his music that he never knew: effects that suddenly come off beyond his expectations. Ecstasy, if it comes at all, will come much later—at a time when he has forgotten all about the work, and then, suddenly hearing it again, he thinks, 'Good lord, did I write that? Why, it isn't so bad after all.'

Most composers feel very foolish when called upon to acknowledge the applause of an enthusiastic audience. It is not that they are ungrateful, or in any way sorry to be approved of and thanked. It is simply that once a work has been completed and seen through its first performance it no longer belongs to the composer. He has sent out his message and other people have received it. Now that the work has left his hands, expressions of gratitude seem irrelevant. He wonders, vaguely, what it has to do with him.

This is not false modesty. He is pleased enough to have written the work, and is doubtless relieved to hear it go down well. But for him the real moments of excitement came when he was composing. This was when the music seemed a living part of himself.

All that belongs to the past. The work must stand on its own feet and there is nothing more he can do. In any case, he is probably battling with a new work and it is this that now seems all-important.

The apparent indifference of composers to the fate of their works sometimes puzzles the ordinary music lover. He hears stories of lost manuscripts, of composers forgetting they have even written certain works, or violently rejecting pieces that displease them. Once he has written the music the composer, it would seem, loses interest. But his attitude is no more peculiar than the kind of detachment the wise parent shows towards his children once they are grown up. If the composer were permanently concerned with the fate of each and every work he would, almost certainly, be unable to write anything new. To him the creation of new music is the only thing that matters—and this, after all, is his reason for living.

Printed by Cox & Wyman Limited
London, Fakenham and Reading